the COOTIE CATCHER BOOK

by the Editors of Klutz

KLUTZ.

Cooties magnified at 1,000,000X.

KLUTZ® is an independent publisher staffed entirely by real human beings. We began our corporate life in 1979 in a garage we shared with a 1962 Chevrolet Impala. Looking back, founders John Cassidy, Darrell Lorentzen and B.C. Rimbeaux are among those who are the most surprised by their improbable success.

Back then, the partners were students, and one of the founding principles for the entire enterprise was thusly stated: Be in and out of business before the end of summer vacation.

So much for that plan.

Plan B? Create the best written, best designed, most imaginative books in the world today. Be honest and fair in all our dealings. Work hard to make every day feel like the first day of summer vacation.
We aim high.

We'd love to hear your comments about this book. **Write us.** •••••••••••••••••••➤

Additional copies

Give us a call at (650) 857-0888 and we'll help track down your nearest Klutz retailer. Should they be out of stock, additional copies of this book, as well as the entire library of 100% Klutz certified books are available in the Klutz catalogue. See the last page for details.

KLUTZ®
455 Portage Ave
Palo Alto, CA 94306

IBSN 1-57054-131-0
4 1 5 8 5 7   www.klutz.com

What's a Cootie Catcher?

Some people call them Fortune Tellers.

They're those little folded paper things that

you open and close with your fingers. Inside

are fortunes like, "You will win the lottery." **or,**

"Your house will soon have a huge swimming pool

in the backyard. Of course, you will have to inflate it."

And, just to prove how powerful we are...

"You will soon turn the page of a small but compelling book..."

How to Fold A Great Looking Cootie Catcher

Any square piece of paper can be made into a Cootie Catcher. But for truly *spectacular* results, we recommend you start with one of our pre-printed Cootie Catcher pages.

1

Tear out a page and place it face down. (Dotted lines up)

Bring the two corners together **exactly**.

Bring the two corners together **exactly**.

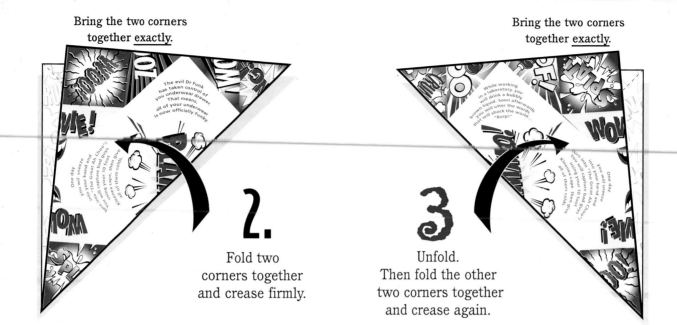

2.
Fold two corners together and crease firmly.

3
Unfold. Then fold the other two corners together and crease again.

Fold each corner point into the center like this.

End up like this.

Keep reading.

Flip the smaller square over.   Then fold all four of these corners into the center.

End up like this.

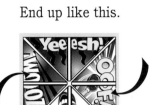

Fold it in half.
This way.

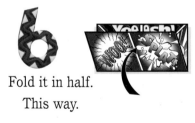

Then unfold, and
fold it in half the
other way.

the big finish

Stick your thumbs and first
two fingers into the four
pockets on the bottom of
the Cootie Catcher.

done!

the Cootie Master

the Player

How to Play

Get your player to **Choose**
one of the top four squares.

If it's a **number,** open and close the Cootie Catcher the right number of times.
For example, the number is 3?
Open and close the Cootie Catcher three times.

Open up and down...   side to side...   and up and down again. ⟶

If your Cootie Catcher has **pictures** on the top (not numbers),
open and close it the right number of letters.

⤎ ·······(The picture is a **Fish**? Open and close four times. F-I-S-H.)

When you've stopped counting, your player should be looking at the inside of your Cootie Catcher. He has to make another choice. He might be looking at numbers. He might be looking at pictures. Whatever he chooses, open and close the Cootie Catcher the right number of times, the same way as before.

When he's finished with that, it's...

Fortune Telling Time

1. **Have him point to one panel.**
2. **Flip up the chosen panel.**
3. **Read the fortune under the panel.**

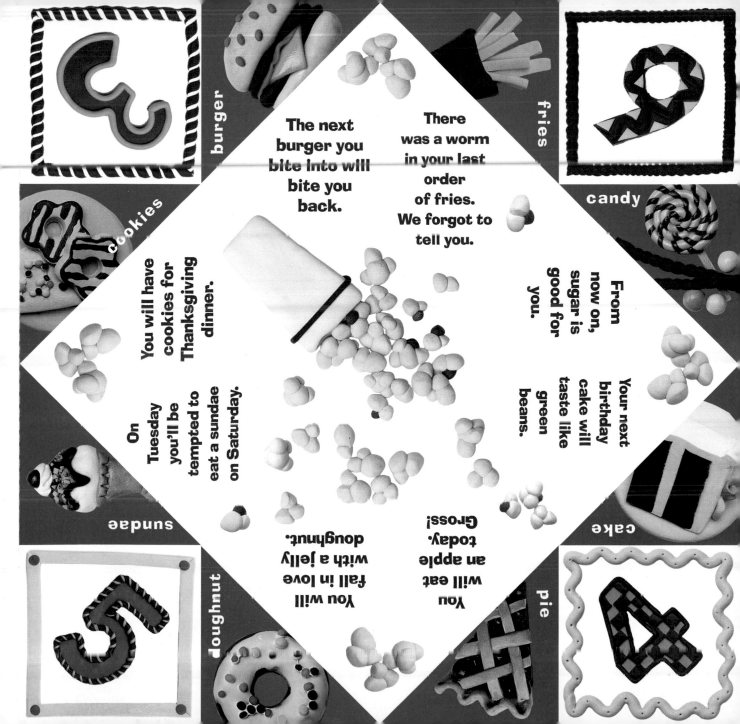

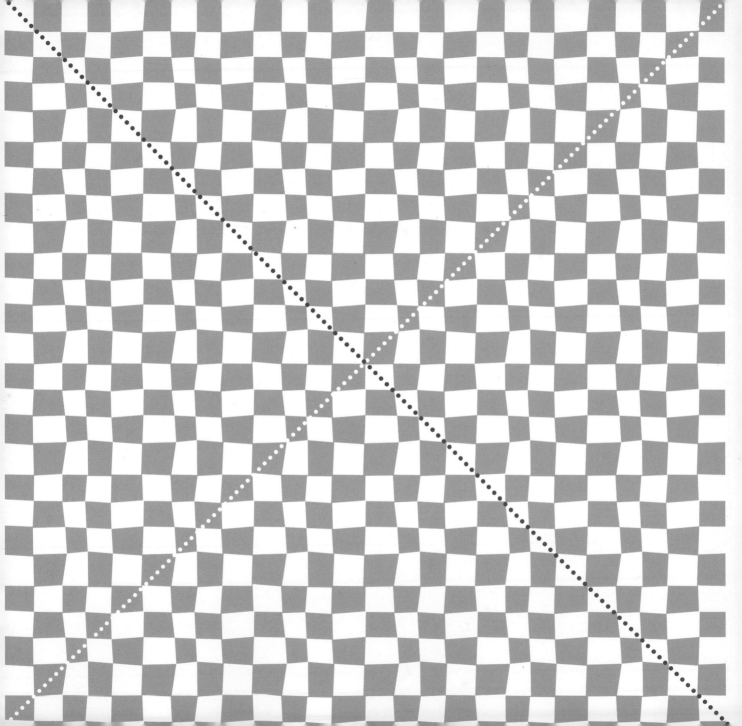

TURTLE

SEAHORSE

JELLYFISH

EEL

Today, you will meet your evil twin.

You will find a quarter in your sink.

You are charming and intelligent.

For the next week, everthing you say will be funny.

You will step on a snail in bare feet.

Your best friend needs to tell you something.

SHARK

CRAB

You are beautiful and brilliant.

You have forgotten something important.

OCTOPUS

FISH

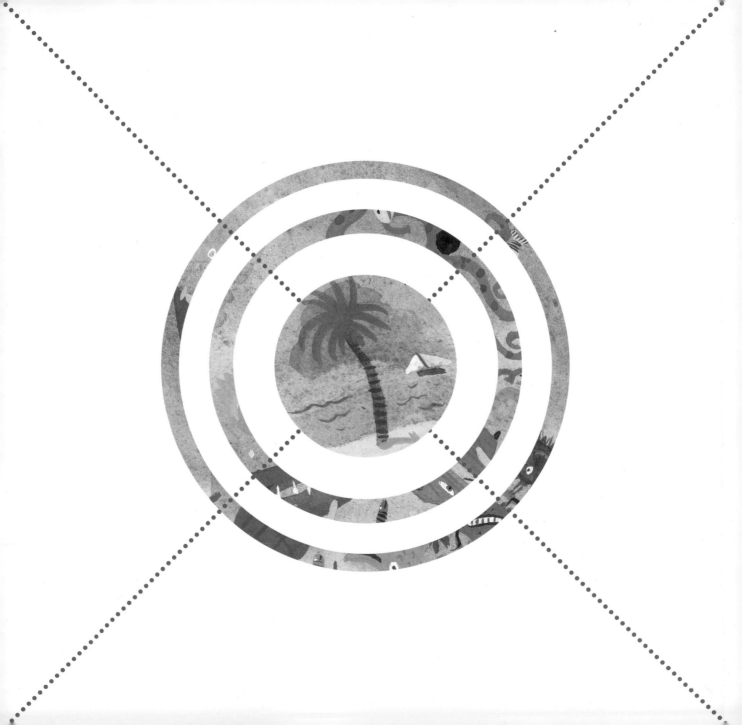

Now, it's your turn.

These next few pages are blank on the inside. Grab a pen and fill them in with some of your own fortunes. Here are a few ideas to get you started.

You will find a lucky bottle cap. • You will get a sunburn on your birthday. • The next time you yawn, a bug will fly into your mouth. • You will walk on the surface of the moon. • You will have twins. • **You will have triplets.** • Your eyes will be closed in your next photograph. • You will soon spill mustard on the person sitting next to you. • You will soon spill ketchup on yourself. Don't wear white. • You will soon catch a cold. • **You will soon go on a long journey**. • You will soon go get me a glass of water and a bag of cookies. And you will hurry back. • **You will fall asleep in your next class.** • The next time you go to sleep, you will dream about elephants. • Your soccer team will elect you "team captain." • In the next game you play, you will score the winning point. • **You will sell your family cow for magic beans.**

more fortunes ➡

When you plant the beans, a huge beanstalk will grow into the sky. You will climb the beanstalk and at the top will be a castle and a Giant. The Giant will be crying because some kid named "Jack" just stole his stuff. • You will like the next vegetable you eat. • You will hate the next vegetable you eat. • Someone will tell you something about your future. • You will fall in love with a tree. • **You will fall in love with a rocking chair.** • You will fall in love with a can of chicken soup. • The President of the United States will call you tonight. He needs your help. • One of your stuffed animals is jealous of your pillow. • You will see a falling star tonight. Be ready to make a wish. • The next time you ride the bus, you will find a rare coin. • **You will be granted three wishes.** • An old friend of yours will soon return what she borrowed. • The next book you read will be turned into a movie. And you will star in the movie. • Someday, your life story will be a movie. • **Tomorrow you will be an inch taller.** • Tomorrow you will be an inch shorter. • The next time you ride your bike, you will get a flat tire. • **The next time you tip in a chair, it will fall over.** • You will be famous. • The next lie you tell will come true. • The next time you lie, you will get caught. • **Your cousin owes you five bucks.** • The next time you go to the bathroom, there will be no toilet paper. • There is a fly in your soup. • You will wear two different shoes to school. • A tree will fall in front of you in the forest and not make a sound. • You   lice of apple pie will taste like cherry pie. • **Listen to the advice of people old**   r bike will be stolen and replaced with the same exact bike. • You will ha   ith many guests from foreign countries. • You will get caught in the rain   school. • **You will bite into an apple and fall into a dee**   eve anything you read in a book. • You will become a magician. • Y   n. • **Your mother's second cousin's daughter's friend Mabel's dog B**   d Eddie has no idea who you are.

fortunes

You can use your Cootie Catcher to read your future in a different way by learning how to play...

M.A.S.H.
Mansion Apartment Shack House

The Set Up: Memorize these five **BIG** questions about your future.

1 Where will you live?

2 Who will you marry?

3 How many kids will you have?

4 What kind of car will you drive?

5 What will be your job?

Then tear out the M.A.S.H. page that looks like this.

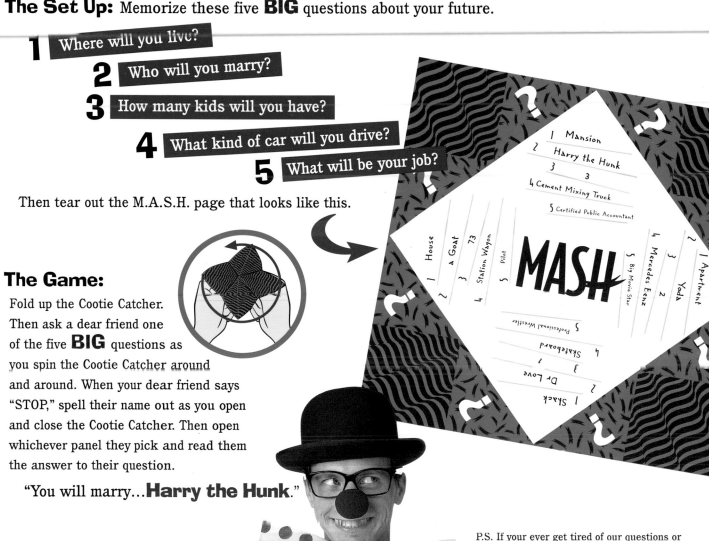

1 Mansion
2 Harry the Hunk
3   3
4 Cement Mixing Truck
5 Certified Public Accountant

1 House
2
3 a Goat
4
5 Station Wagon
73
5 Pilot

MASH

1 Apartment
2
3 Yoda
4 Mercedes Benz
5 Big Movie Star

1 Shack
2
3 Dr. Love
4 Skateboard
5 Professional Wrestler

The Game:

Fold up the Cootie Catcher. Then ask a dear friend one of the five **BIG** questions as you spin the Cootie Catcher around and around. When your dear friend says "STOP," spell their name out as you open and close the Cootie Catcher. Then open whichever panel they pick and read them the answer to their question.

"You will marry...**Harry the Hunk**."

P.S. If your ever get tired of our questions or answers, write some of your own. We've provided three blank Cootie Catchers for you to use.

Your future is nice. But let's hear about your past.

Or better still your present. How about a little...

TRUTH or DARE!

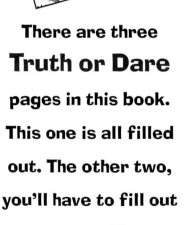

Step 1
Tear out this page and fold it up.

Step 2
Stand in front of a dear friend and spin your Cootie Catcher until they say "STOP".

Open and close the Cootie Catcher as you spell their name.

Step 3
When you're done spelling, your friend will be looking at four choices — Truths or Dares. They must pick one. When they do, flip the panel and read it.

The KILLER BIG Rule:
If they choose "truth," then become too shy to tell the truth, they **MUST** do the dare.
If they choose "dare," then become too chicken to do the dare, they **MUST** tell the truth.

There are three Truth or Dare pages in this book. This one is all filled out. The other two, you'll have to fill out yourself.

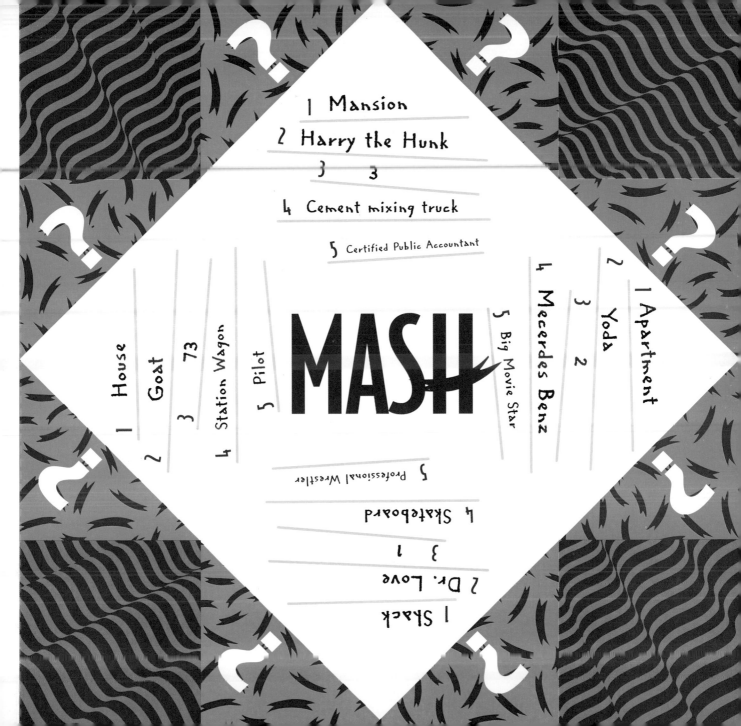

MASH

1 Mansion
2 Harry the Hunk
3 _____ 3
4 Cement mixing truck
5 Certified Public Accountant

1 Apartment
2 Yoda
3 2
4 Mecerdes Benz
5 Big Movie Star

1 House
2 Goat
3 73
4 Station Wagon
5 Pilot

1 Shack
2 Dr. Love
3 1
4 Skateboard
5 Professional Wrestler

truth or DARE!

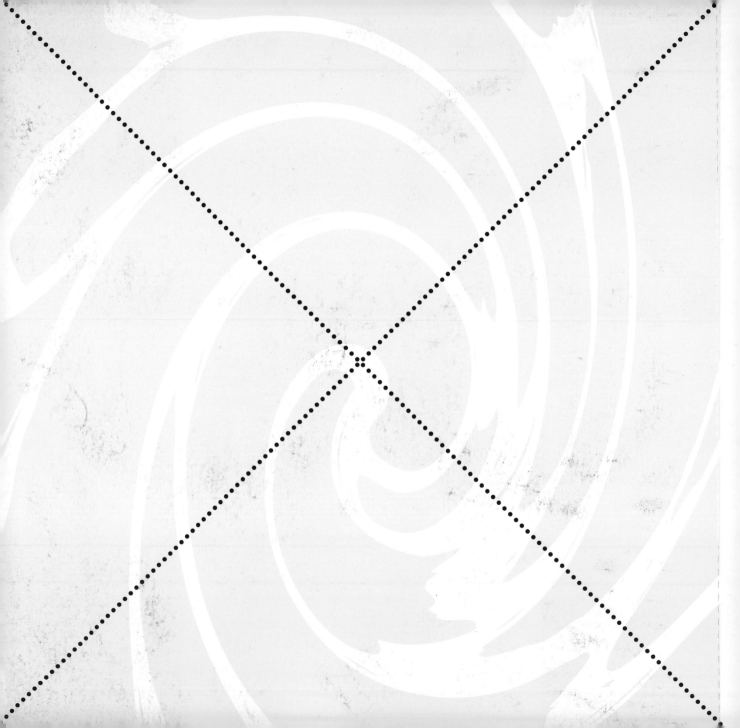

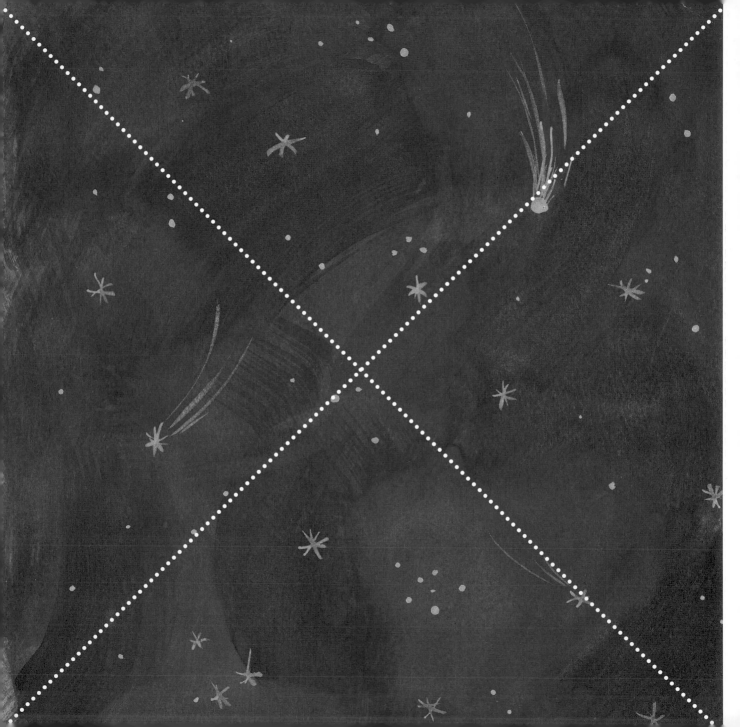

truth

dare

dare

truth

truth

dare

truth

dare

Describe your dream date.

Suck on your thumb for the next minute.

Show us the Wubba Wubba dance.

What color is your underwear?

Free pass. Ask someone else a question.

Sing a short opera about what you did today.

truth or dare

If you could, what would you change about yourself?

Count to 10, like a duck.

1 _____

2 _____

3 _____

4 _____

5 _____

MASH

5 _____

4 _____

3 _____

2 _____

1 _____

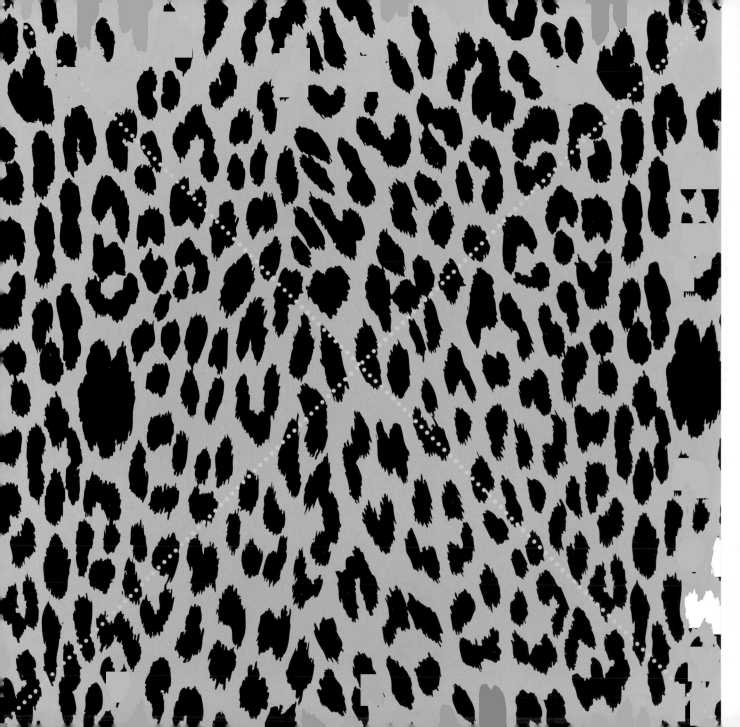

MASH

1 _____
2 _____
3 _____
4 _____
5 _____

1
2
3
4
5

5 4 3 2 1

5 4 3 2 1

1 _____
2 _____
3 _____
4 _____
5 _____

Here are the
Official Rules
to

cootie Catching

(This is the game, incidentally, that gave Cootie Catchers their name.)

1. Fold your Cootie Catcher the regular way.

2. When you're done, open and close it a few times (a test run).
Opened one way it will be clean white. Opened the other,
it will be full of disgusting bugs.

3. Approach a beloved friend or relative. Show them the clean white inside of your Cootie Catcher.
Make them shake their hair over it. Tell them that you're trying to catch
any tiny micro-organisms that might fall out of their hair.
As you bring the Cootie Catcher back to look at your "catch,"
turn a bit so they can't see you
and open the Cootie Catcher the other way.

4. Stare at the horrible bugs and scream.
Then show your friend.

p.s. For even better results
sprinkle in some REAL sand or dirt into the
bugs part before you start.

Turn Any Piece of Paper Into A Cootie Catcher

Regular Typing Paper

1

2 Fold one corner like this.

3 Tear off the uncovered part.

4 Unfold. You've got a square.

Paper Towels

The Yellow Pages

Old Shopping Bags

Wrapping Paper

Toilet Paper
(Already comes in ready-to-use squares)

Cootie Funnies

Cootie Money

FOLD   FOLD

A perfect square.
Now you're ready to fold.

Cootie Credits

Art Direction:
Mary Ellen Podgorski

Book Design:
Michael Sherman

Photography:
Peter Fox

Needless Delays:
John Cassidy

Thanks to **Laura Torres**.

Models:
Kaela Fox
Jenner Fox
Katherine Daiss
Genevieve Yang
Jay Houston Yang
Kaja Martin
Veronica Dolan
Sean Hurlburt
Alicia Edelman

DeWitt Durham
Kate Krislov
Michael Sherman
Kathy Harrington
Mark Judge
Chriss Miller

Corie Thompson
Bill Olson
Wendy Jacobsen
Marilyn Green
Jeff Hill
Domino

"Clay Food"
Sherri Haab

"Dogs"
Michael Scanlan

"Jungle"
Jannine Cabossel

"Bang"
Michael Sherman

"Pizza"
Margaret Spengler

"Flowers"
Melanie Marder Parks

"Cards"
Michael Sherman

Illustrators

"Tropical Island"
Jesse Hartland

"Pets"
Lori Osieki

"Fruits & Veggies"
Tatjana Krizmanic

"Witches"
Jeff Seaver

"Stuff"
Mary Thelan

Stars "M.A.S.H."
Mary Ellen Podgorski

Bugs "Truth or Dare"
Elwood H Smith

Flowers "M.A.S.H."
Tatjana Krizmanic

Write Us:

We want to hear your comments about this, or any other Klutz book. We've even given you a postcard to make it easy. We always read all our mail. You can also use this card to get a copy of the Klutz Catalogue — a complete listing of all the fine books we publish. Here's how you do it:

1. **Cut out.**
2. **Fill in.**
3. **Add stamp.**
4. **Mail (Important)**
5. **Wait impatiently.**

Who are you?

Name: _____

Address: _____

City: _____ State: _____ Zip: _____

How did you first hear about this book? _____

Draw a picture of yourself here ↘

Tell us what you think of this book:

_____

_____

_____

_____

_____

_____

What would you like us to write a book about? _____

❑ Check this box of you want us to send you The Klutz Catalogue

The Cootie Catcher Book

More Great Books From **KLUTZ**.

Bubble Gum Science

The Buck Book

Cat's Cradle

You Can Make A Collage

Chinese Jump Rope

The Incredible Clay Book

The Etch A Sketch Book

Friendship Bracelets

The Official Icky-Poo Book

The Klutz Book of Jacks

Draw the Marvel Comics™ Super Heroes™

Nail Art

Pipe Cleaners Gone Crazy

The Most Incredible Sticker Book You've Ever Seen

Stop the Watch

Table Top Football

Kids Travel

The Klutz Yo-Yo

KLUTZ®

455 Portage Avenue

Palo Alto, CA 94306

First
Class
Postage
Here